What the Dog Saw

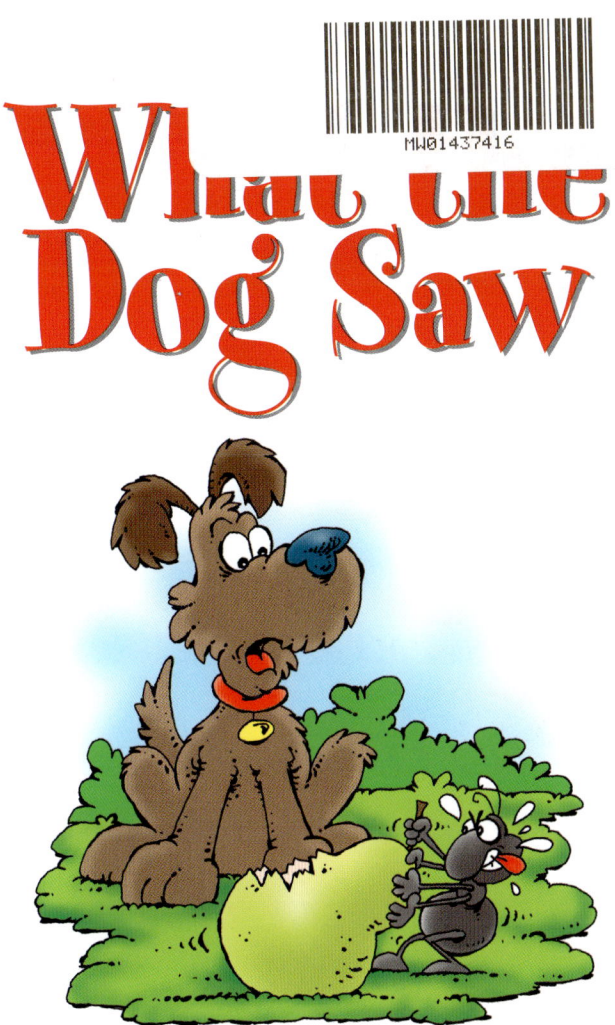

by Gregory Grissom
illustrated by Mike Dammer

Editorial Offices: Glenview, Illinois • Parsippany, New Jersey • New York, New York
Sales Offices: Needham, Massachusetts • Duluth, Georgia • Glenview, Illinois
Coppell, Texas • Ontario, California • Mesa, Arizona

Every effort has been made to secure permission and provide appropriate credit for photographic material. The publisher deeply regrets any omission and pledges to correct errors called to its attention in subsequent editions.

Unless otherwise acknowledged, all photographs are the property of Scott Foresman, a division of Pearson Education.

ISBN: 0-328-13214-4

Copyright © Pearson Education, Inc.

All Rights Reserved. Printed in the United States of America. This publication is protected by Copyright, and permission should be obtained from the publisher prior to any prohibited reproduction, storage in a retrieval system, or transmission in any form by any means, electronic, mechanical, photocopying, recording, or likewise. For information regarding permission(s), write to: Permissions Department, Scott Foresman, 1900 East Lake Avenue, Glenview, Illinois 60025.

3 4 5 6 7 8 9 10 V010 14 13 12 11 10 09 08 07 06

Hi! My name is Brown. Can you guess why that is my name?

I live behind the house. All kinds of things go on out here. Watch with me.

Look at the squirrel!
His arms are full of nuts. I have never seen so many nuts. What makes his cheeks so round? Nuts!
Wow! He must be hungry!

Look at that ant.
What is she pulling along? It is very big. It is a huge pear!
Wow! She must be hungry!

Look at that bird.
That bird found an apple. She is flying toward her nest. Look at her eyes! Is the apple too heavy?
Wow! She must be hungry.

When I am hungry, my owner puts out food! I am a lucky dog!
Thanks for visiting. I will eat now.

Plants and Animals Work Together

Plants and animals help each other. Plants and animals keep each other alive!

Plants help the animals. Squirrels like to eat nuts and seeds. Ants like to eat fruit and sweet things. Birds like fruit and seeds.

Animals also help the plants. Animals carry seeds around. They drop seeds all over the place. The seeds grow into plants. Animals help make sure that plants grow in lots of places!